Electric Fantasy © Daniel Pelavin 2010. All rights reserved

The models and renderings in this book were created in Adobe Dimensions v 3.0 during the months of April through November 2007 in an effort to extend the boundaries of a simple, but deceptively powerful 3D rendering, modeling and animation program which Adobe supported from 1994 until its "End of Life" on November 16, 2004 (July 19, 2005 in Japan). A dimensional modeling feature was added to Adobe Illustrator beginning with v 11.0, Illustrator CS, however, functionality is limited to modeling single objects rather than complete scenes, processing is slow and mapping is an awkward and complicated affair.

Dimensions offered a robust set of modeling tools including extruding and revolving editable paths and bevels, but very limited tools to manipulate or modify shapes once they were formed. Lighting and shading options were meager compared to even the most modest of entry-level programs today, however, underlying the simplistic interface was a sturdy mesh-based modeling framework that could, with great patience and modest effort, be coaxed into producing some sophisticated effects.

The introduction of Apple Mac OS X v 10.5, which no longer supported the Classic environment, sounded the final death knell for Adobe Dimensions, though existing copies can still be used in imaginative ways on older systems.

Contents

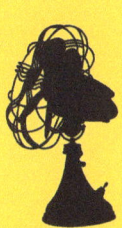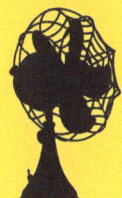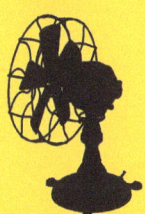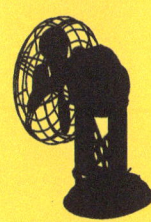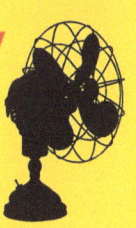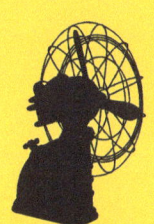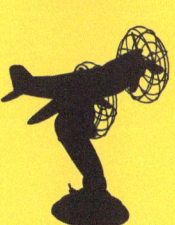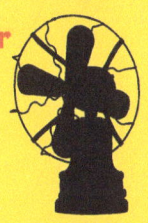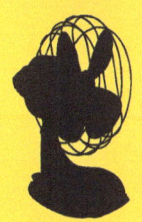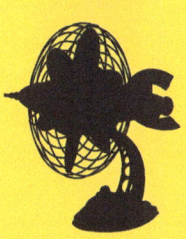

In the steamy Detroit summers of the mid-1950s, I would sit
with my dad on our back porch, radio tuned to the action at
Briggs Stadium as Al Kaline lead the Tigers to another win.
Our respite from the heat, a green electric fan, oscillating
from side to side with poise and dignity. Its streamlined shape,
regal shield and gentle hum made it a magical presence as it
embraced us in gentle breezes. It has remained a fond memory
and inspiration for the whimsical fans of my imagination.

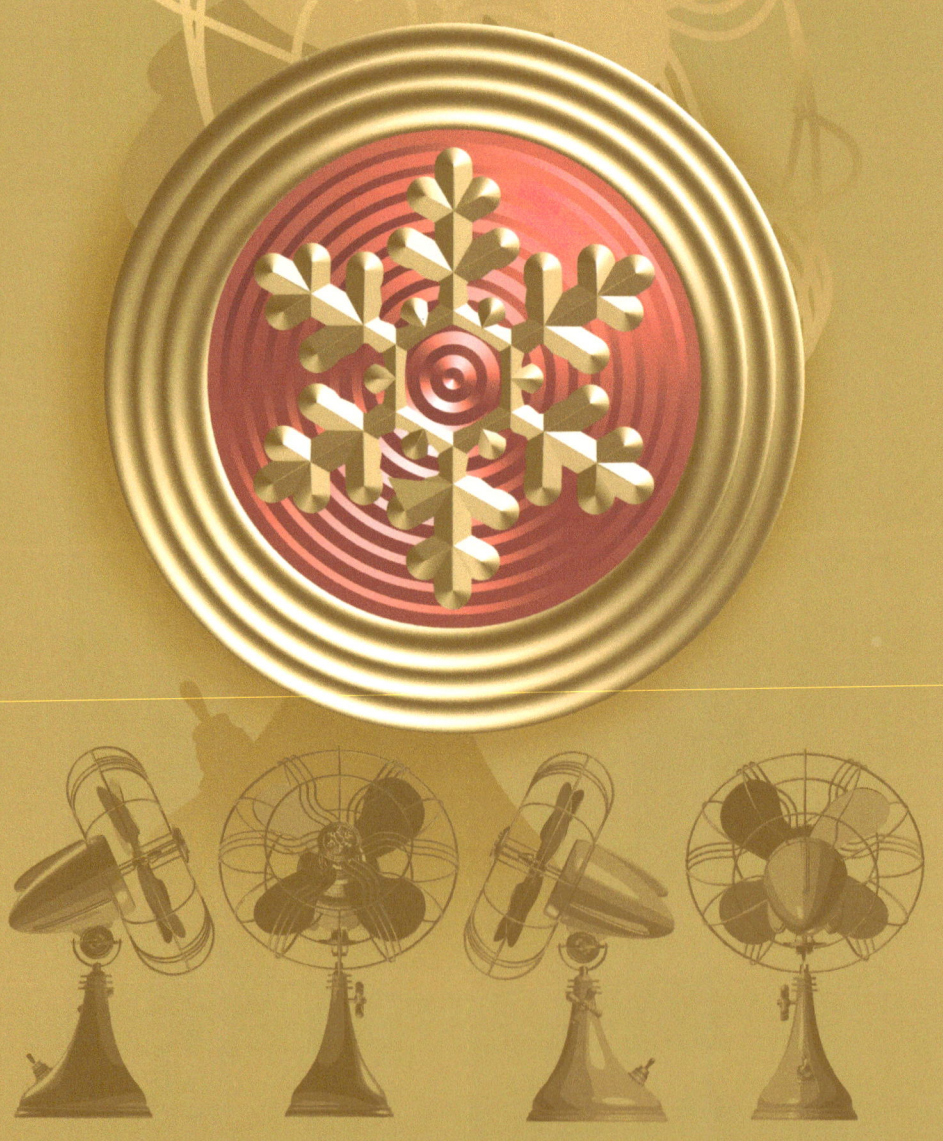

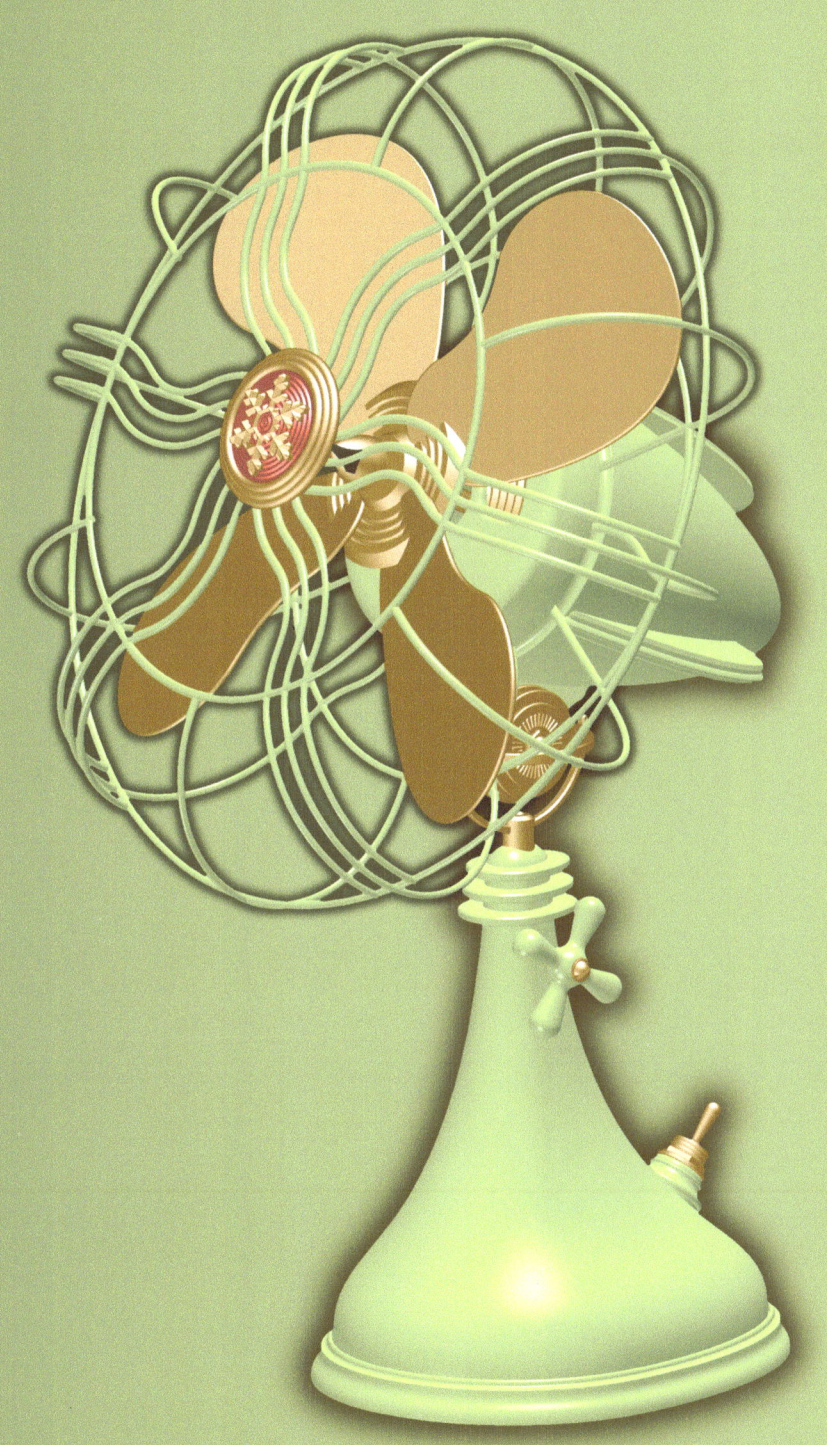

A nine-spoked grill fashioned after the classic orb web and five copper blades with scalloped trailing edges distinguish the Spider from the quotidian peers of its day. Rising from an hexagonal encasement, a matching copper pivot mechanism supports a shaded pole uni/poly-phase AC induction motor. The graceful teardrop base and motor casing are accented with pearlescent taupe control knobs while an ebony replica of its namesake keeps a serene vigil over her domain ensconced majestically atop an escutcheon with gold fresnel reflector.

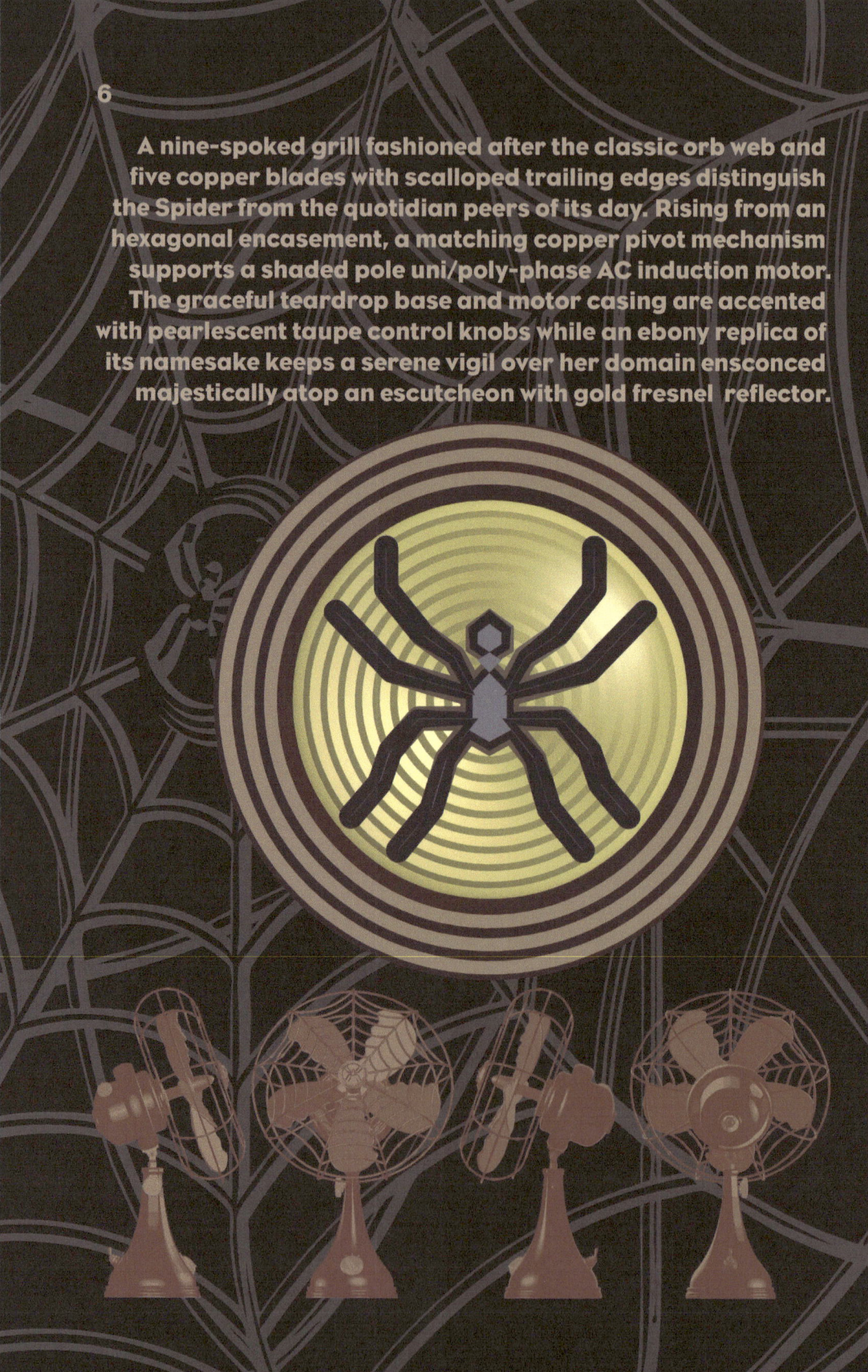

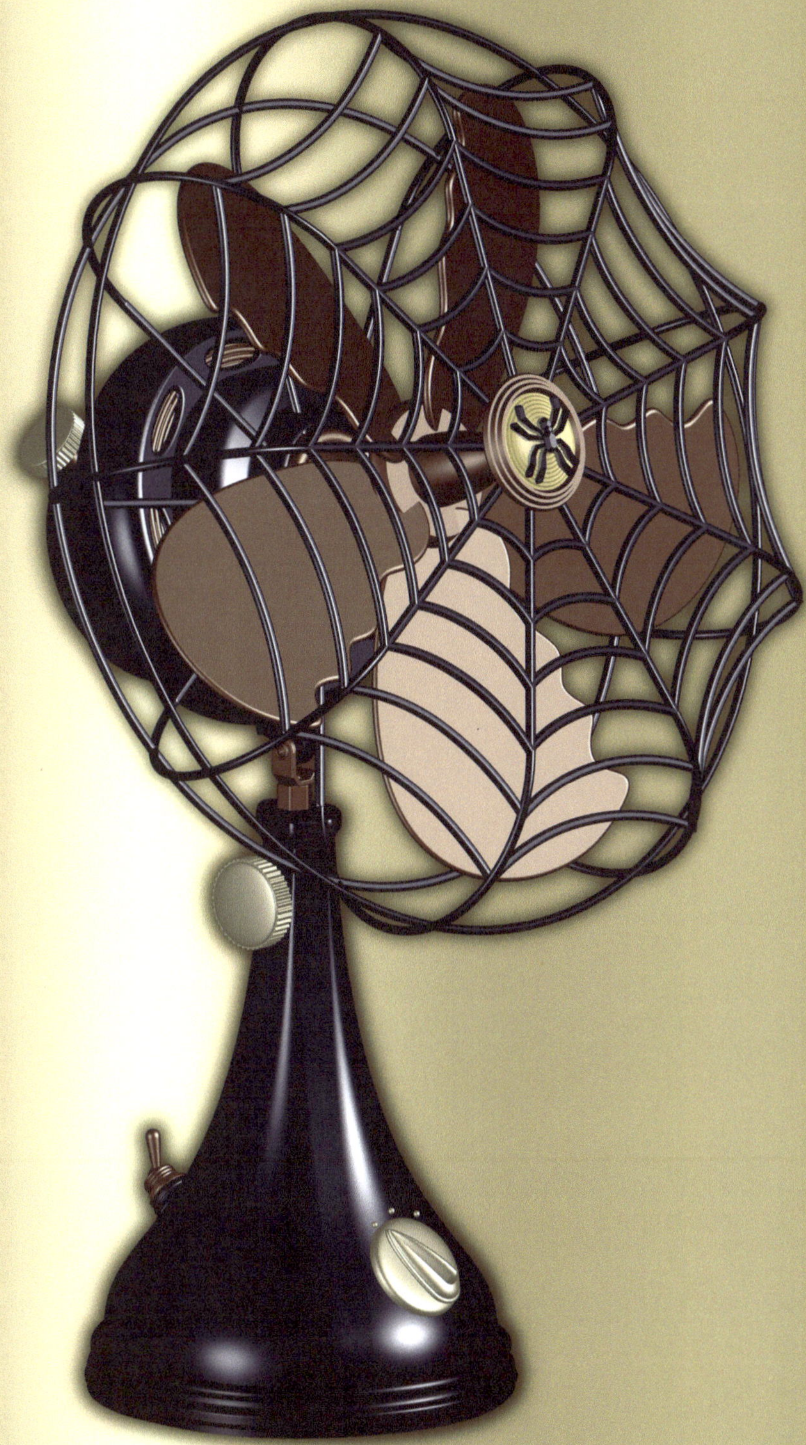

With the crackling of sparks and blades whirring through air pungent with the sweet smell of electricity, the first practical personal fans came into use in the 1890s. Perched on sturdy claw feet, the "centrifugal air pump" harnessed the mysterious forces of magnetism and heralded the genesis of commercial electrical power. Vernacular construction enhanced by a stylistic vocabulary germane to the era helped meld form with function into objects of cultivated beauty which endures today.

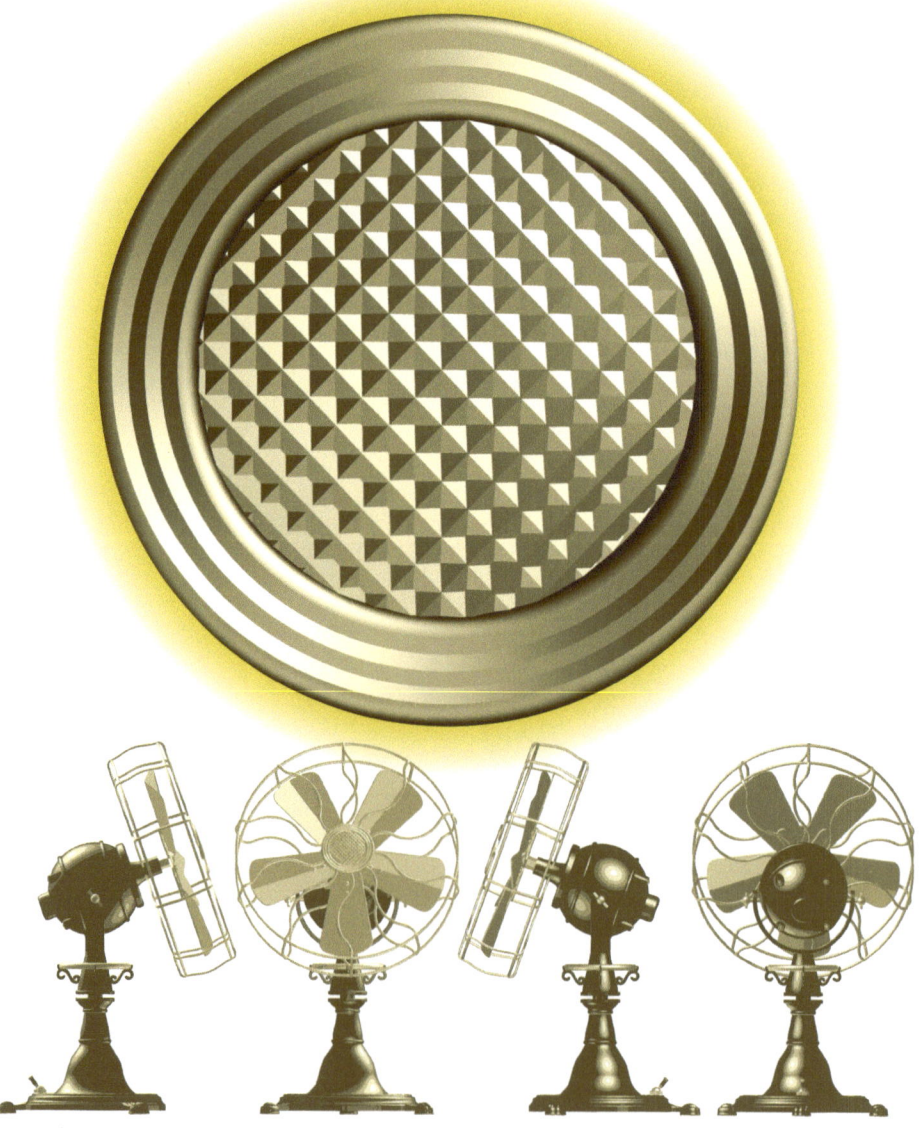

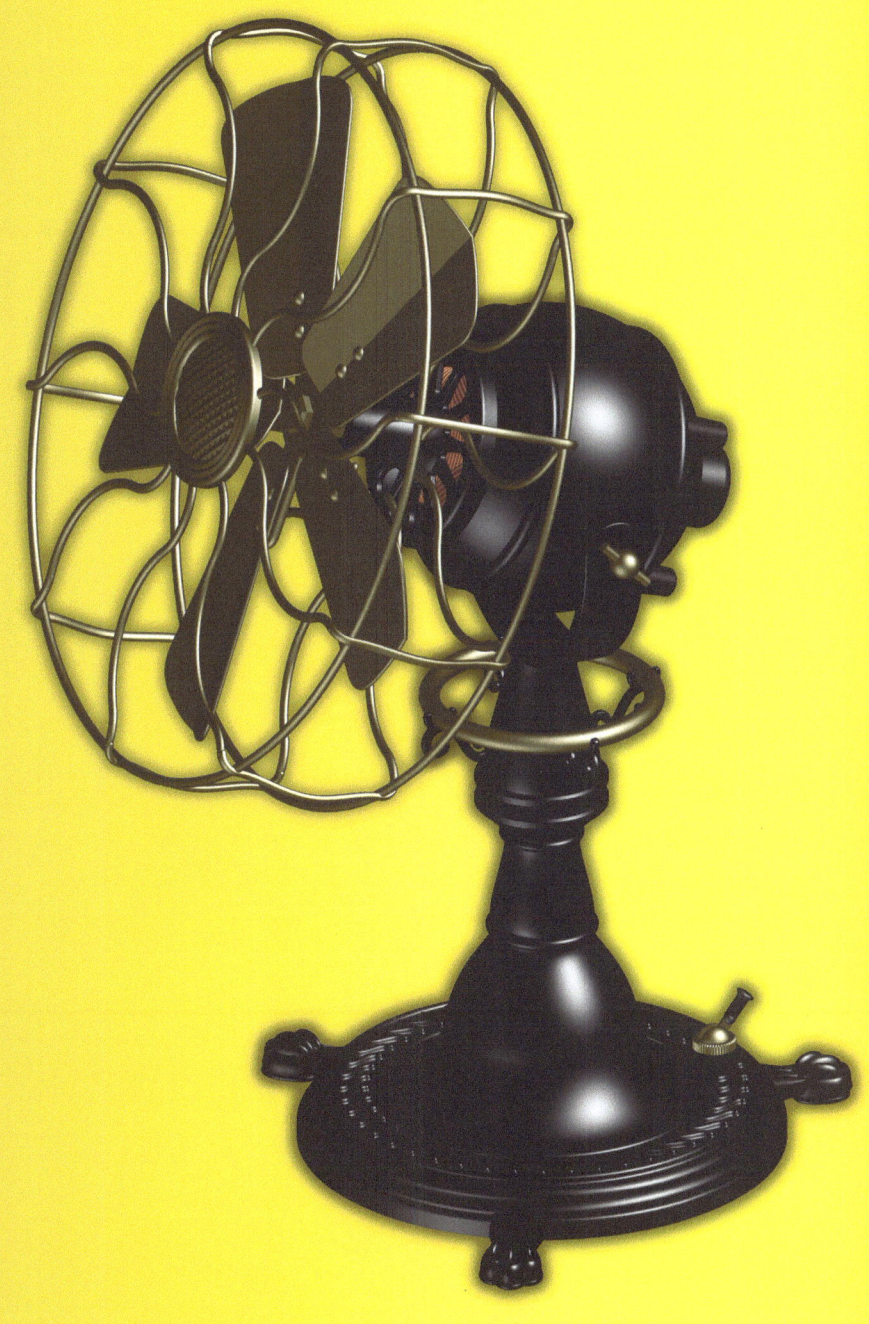

This unusual alternate form factor prototype uses a rotating cross-braced frame from which the motor is suspended. Oscillation is achieved through means of an hydraulically assisted swivel mechanism positioned at its base while the horizontal adjustment of the motor, blade and aluminum cage assembly is accomplished through adjustable tension knobs on either side of the motor mounts. A three-way top-mounted pilot light provides a visual indication of fan speed.

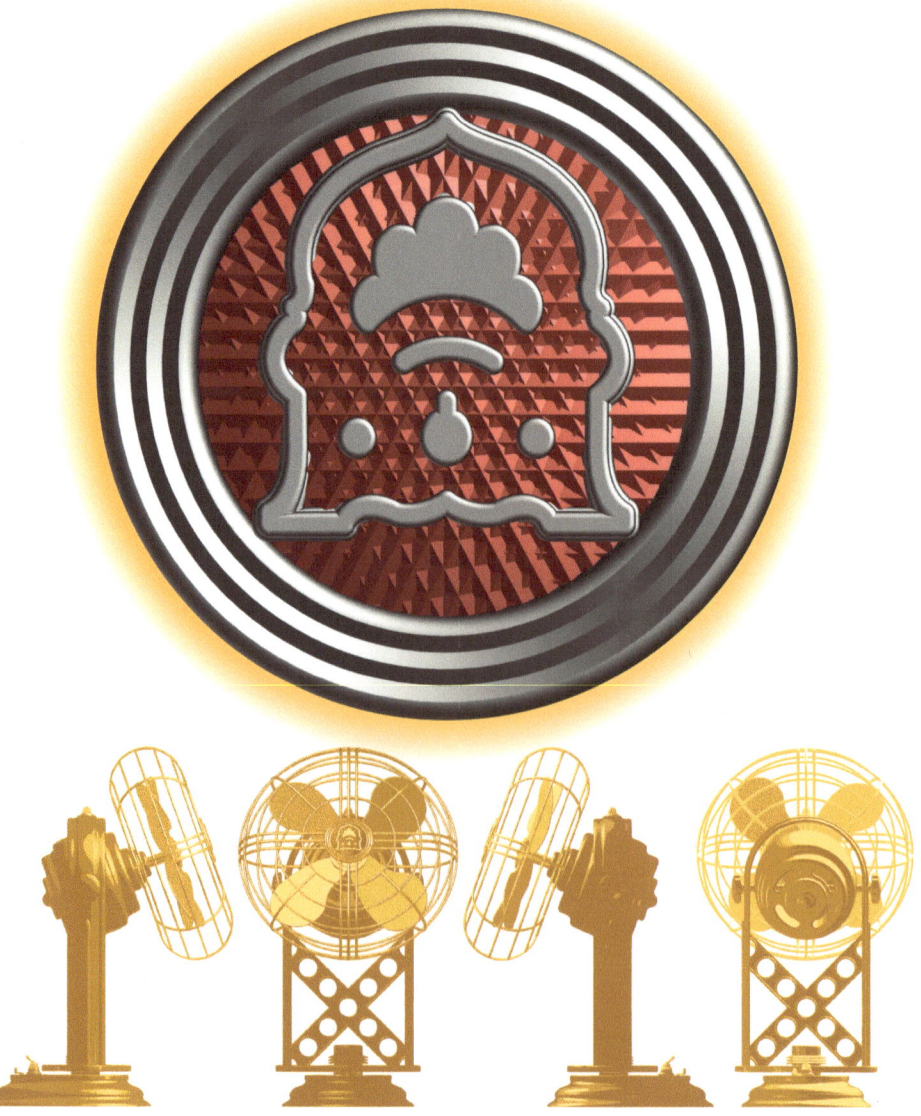

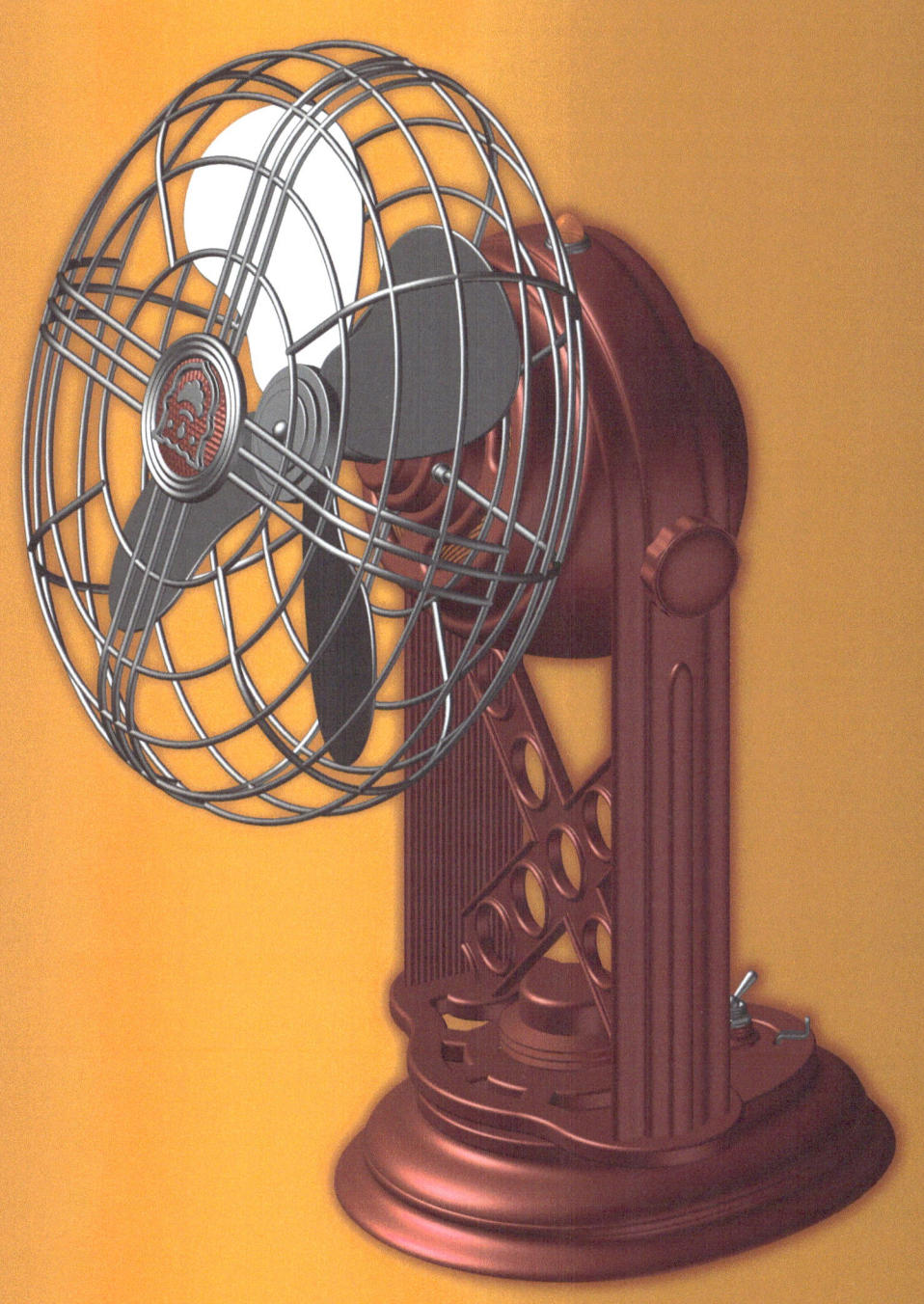

With its focus on the heavens and beyond, this fan features a unique vertically mounted motor which controls both rotation and oscillation. Self-lubricating articulated bevel gears transfer the power to the blade shaft which is completely adjustable through a range of 90° from horizontal to vertical and enclosed in a dome-shaped housing reminiscent of an observatory telescope shutter mechanism. The cosmic theme is carried through to a badge bearing planets of the Solar System.

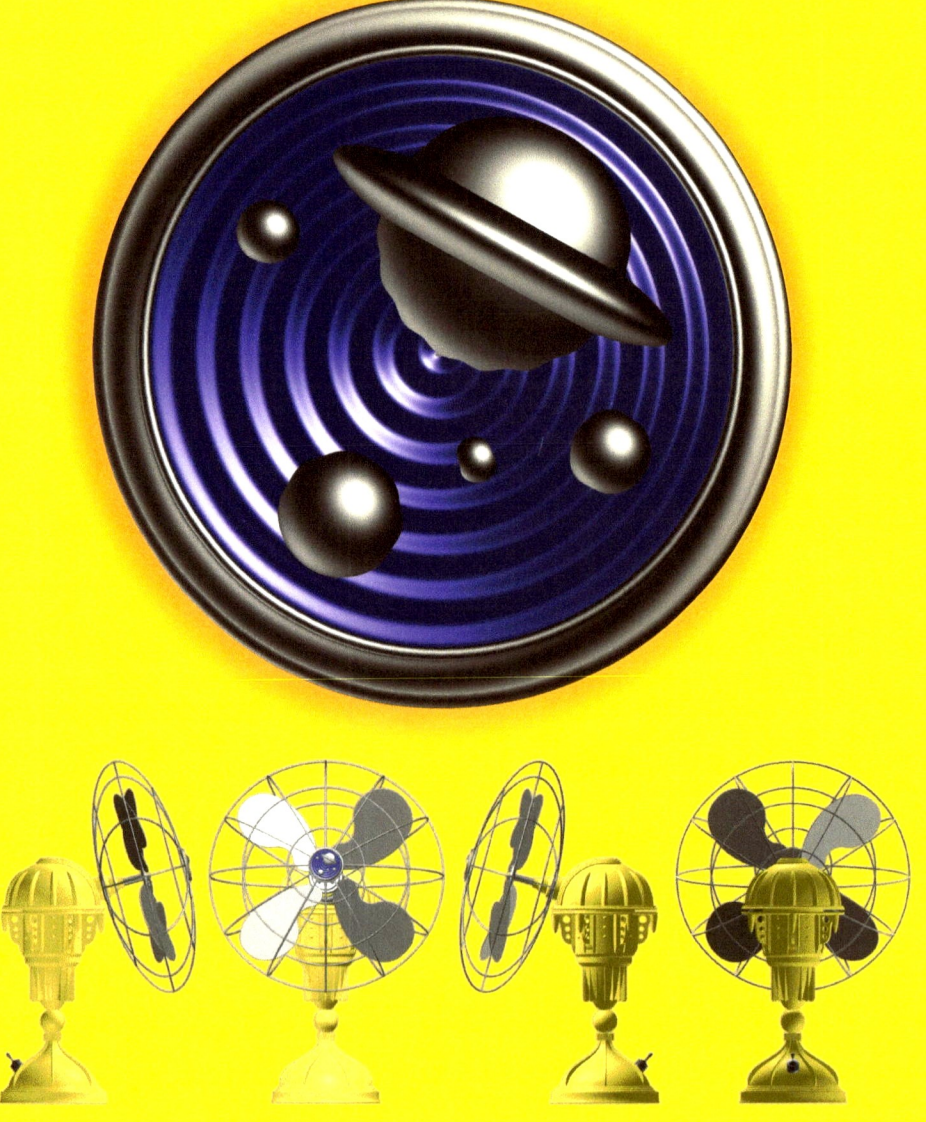

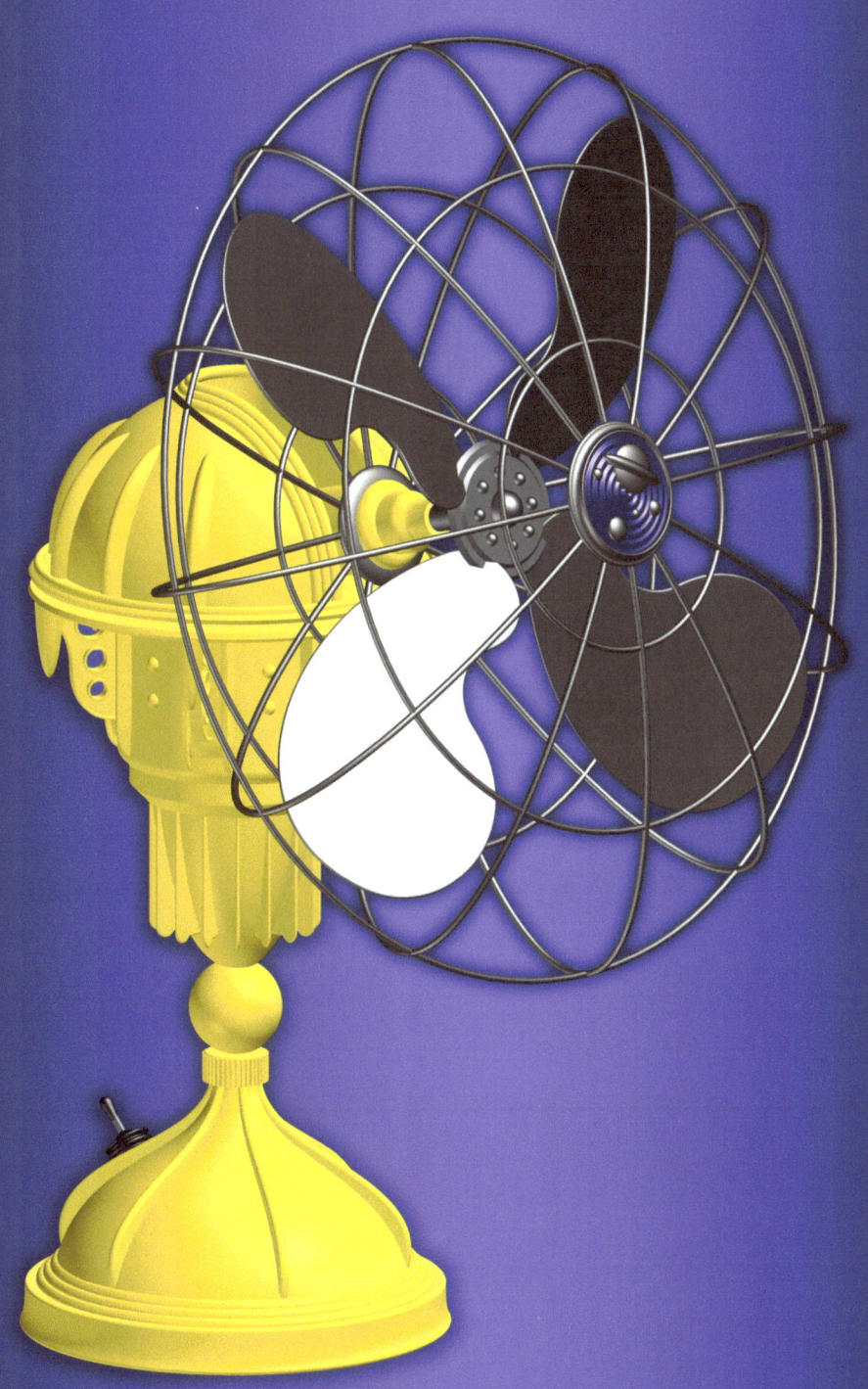

Exploring the subtle relationship between fans and propeller craft, the biplane is a celebration of an early icon of man's quest to conquer the sky. Perched delicately on a streamlined base by twin-strut landing gear, a stylized fuselage serves as the motor housing. Protruding nobly from an exaggerated cowling are blades with the distinctive pitch and contours of an aircraft propeller. Aviation style throttle handles serve as power switch and speed control lever and the horizontal directional alignment is adjusted along the axis of the tires.

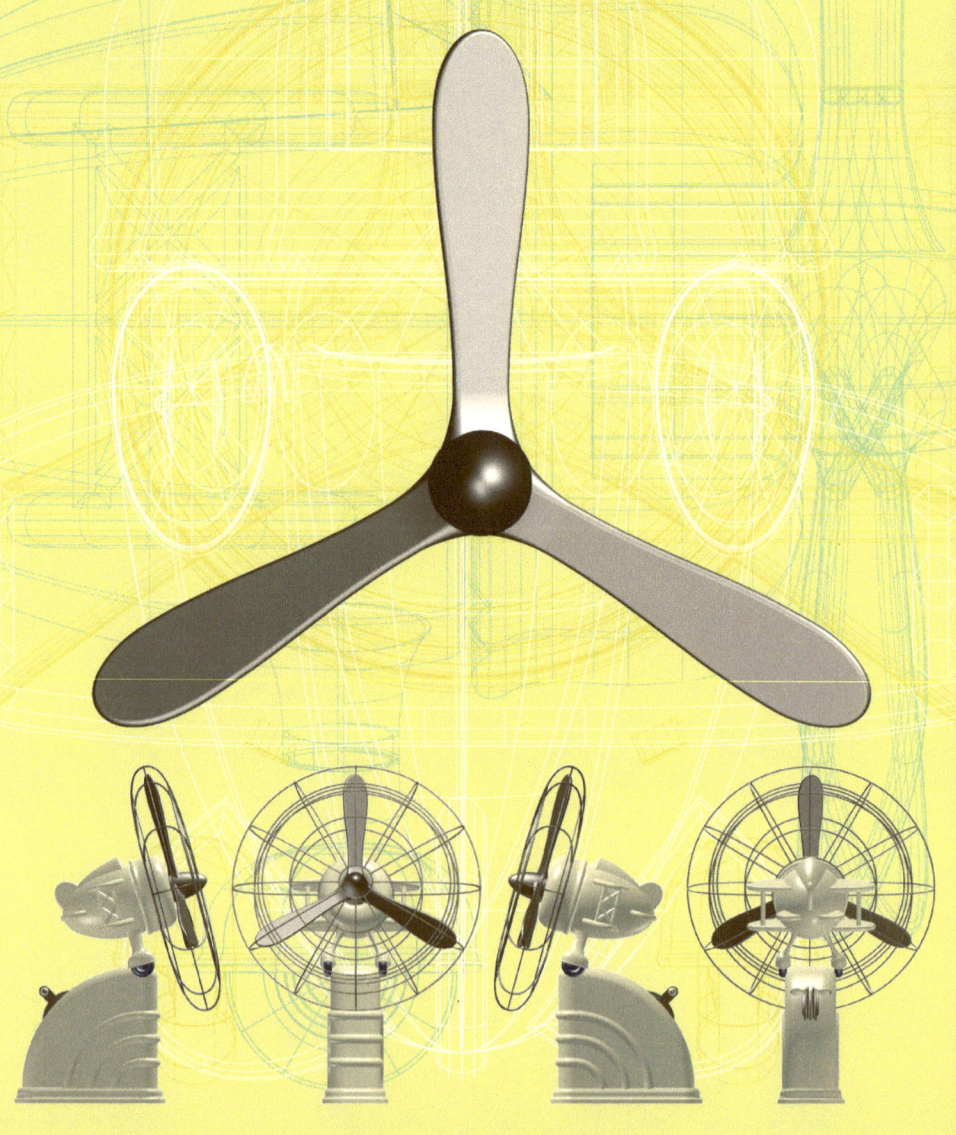

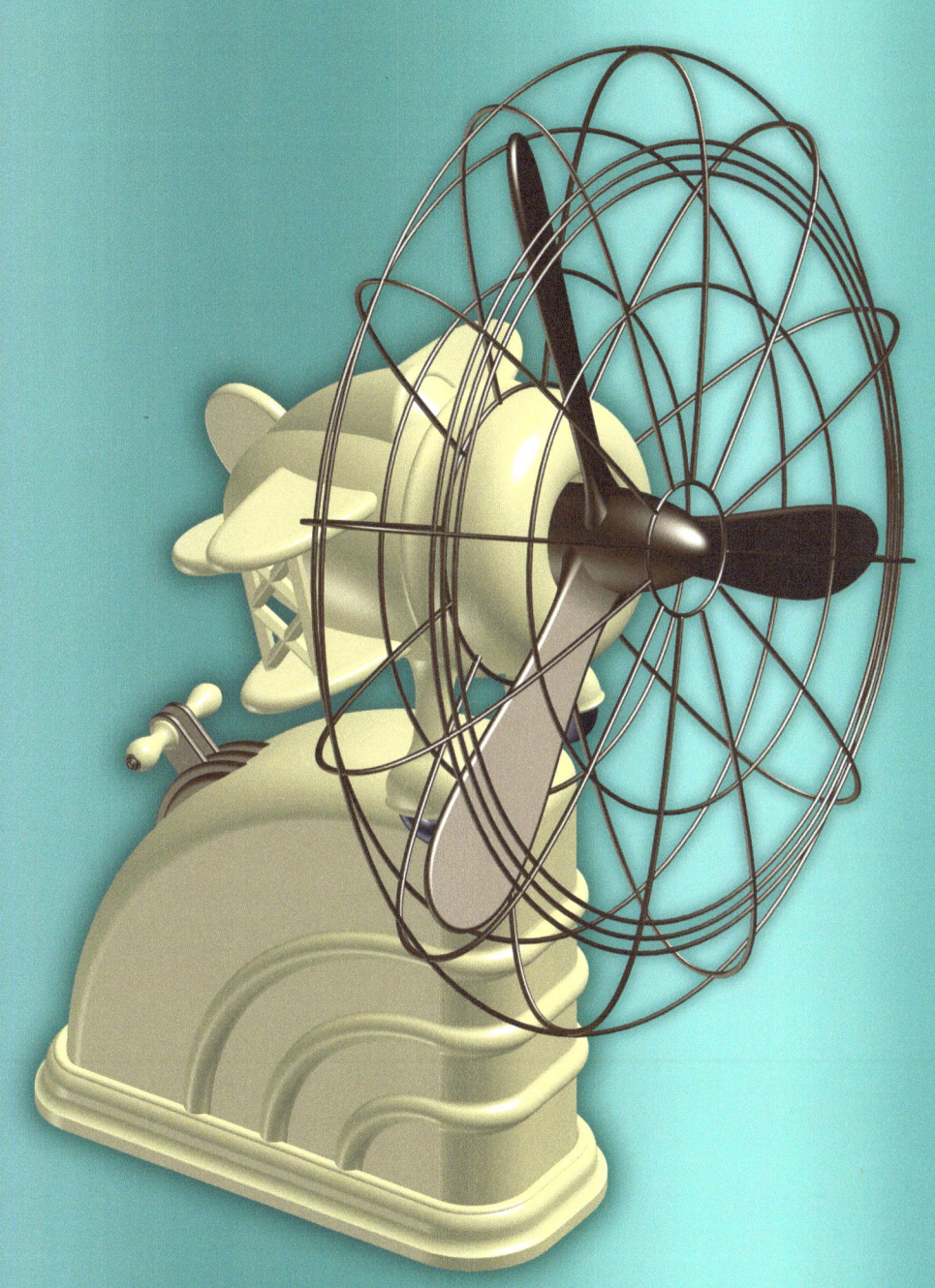

First flown over 75 years ago, the Douglas DC-3, certainly the greatest airliner of its time and even, some would say, of all time, marked a turning point that made commercial air transportation possible. In use by over 30 airlines at its peak in 1939 and, in even greater numbers for military transport as the C-47, some still fly today in service around the globe. A gleaming silver facsimile with twin motors and opposed blades pays homage to this esteemed veteran of the skies. Discreetly housed in the translucent nose: a softly glowing night light.

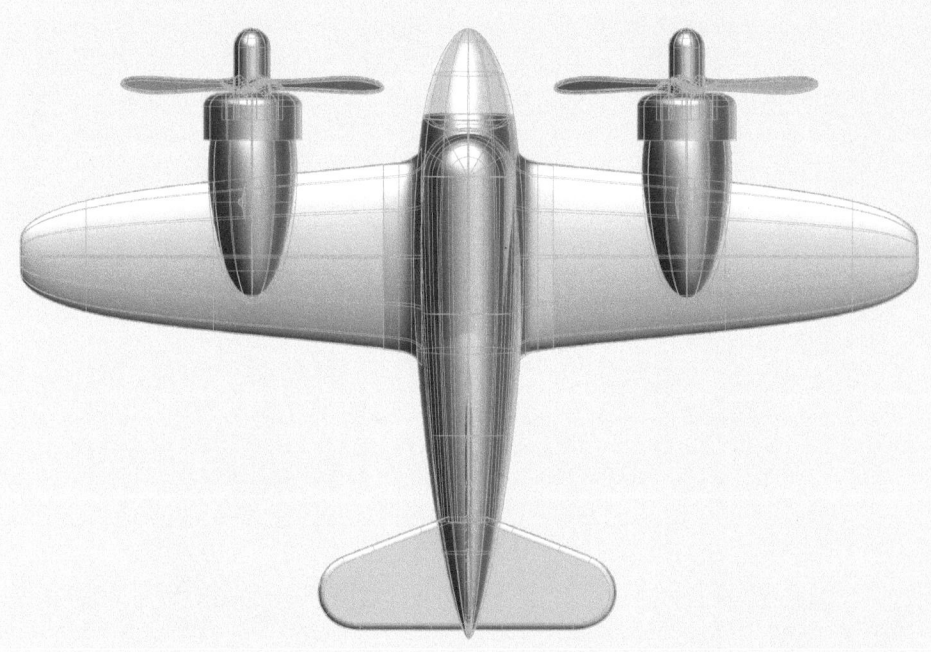

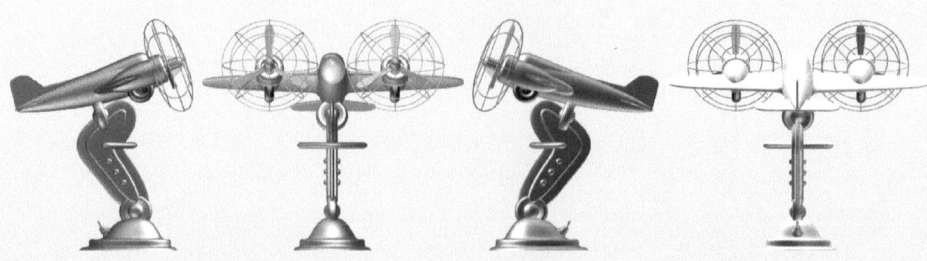

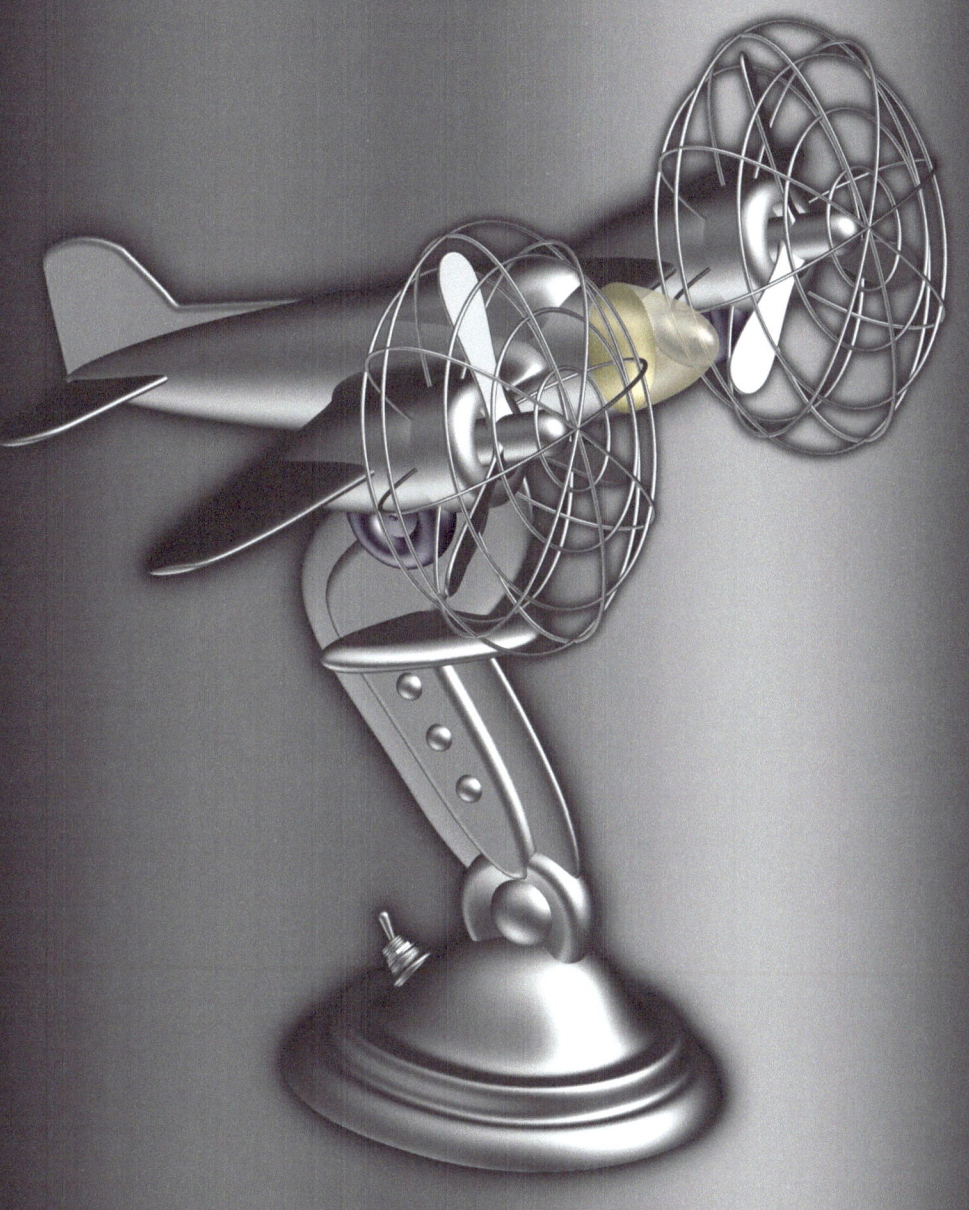

Reality meets fantasy in this accurate rendering of an actual tischventilator (table fan). No liberties were taken in the reproduction of what most certainly was a formidable appliance in its day. It's probably fair to assume this hefty hunk of cast iron and brass was not likely to vibrate and shimmy away from its assigned location. One can almost feel the palpable and exacting click as a turn of the precision switch set this behemoth lurching powerfully into motion.

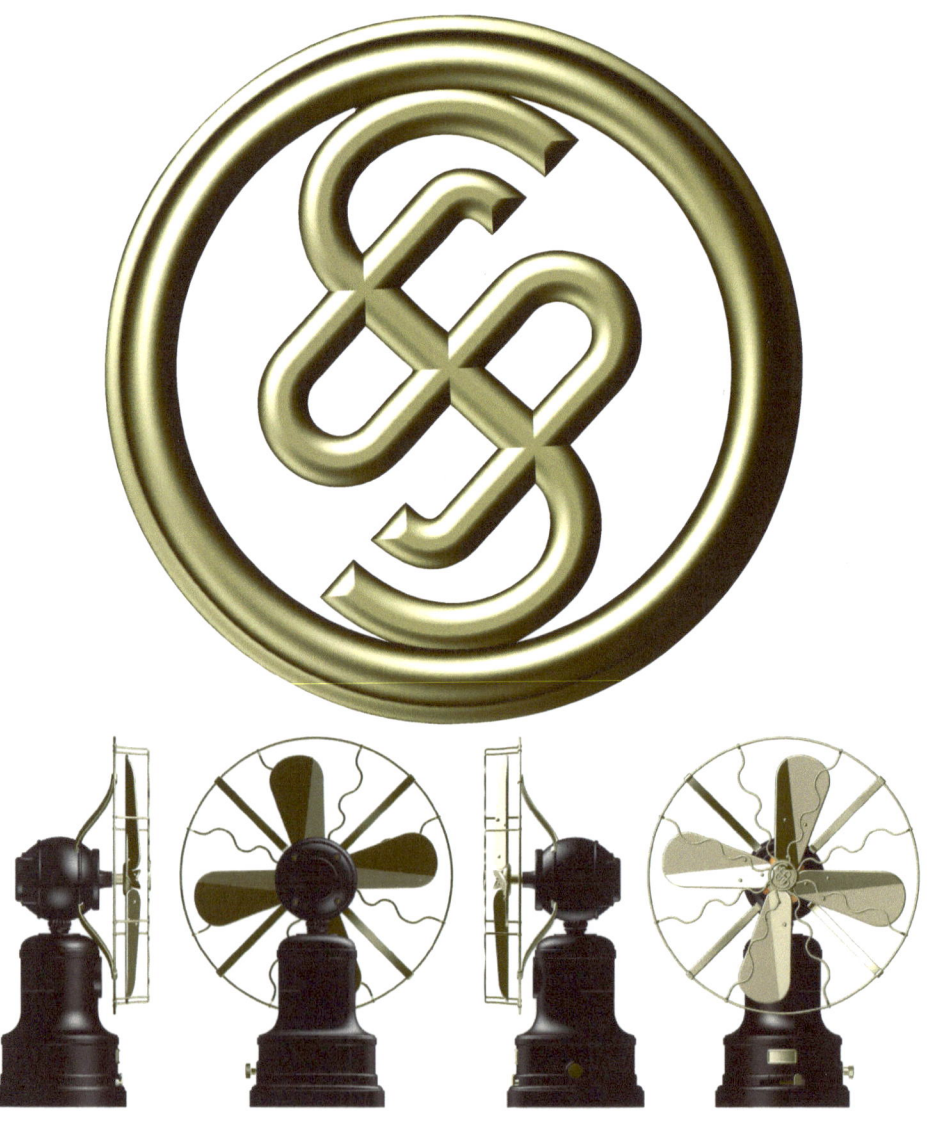

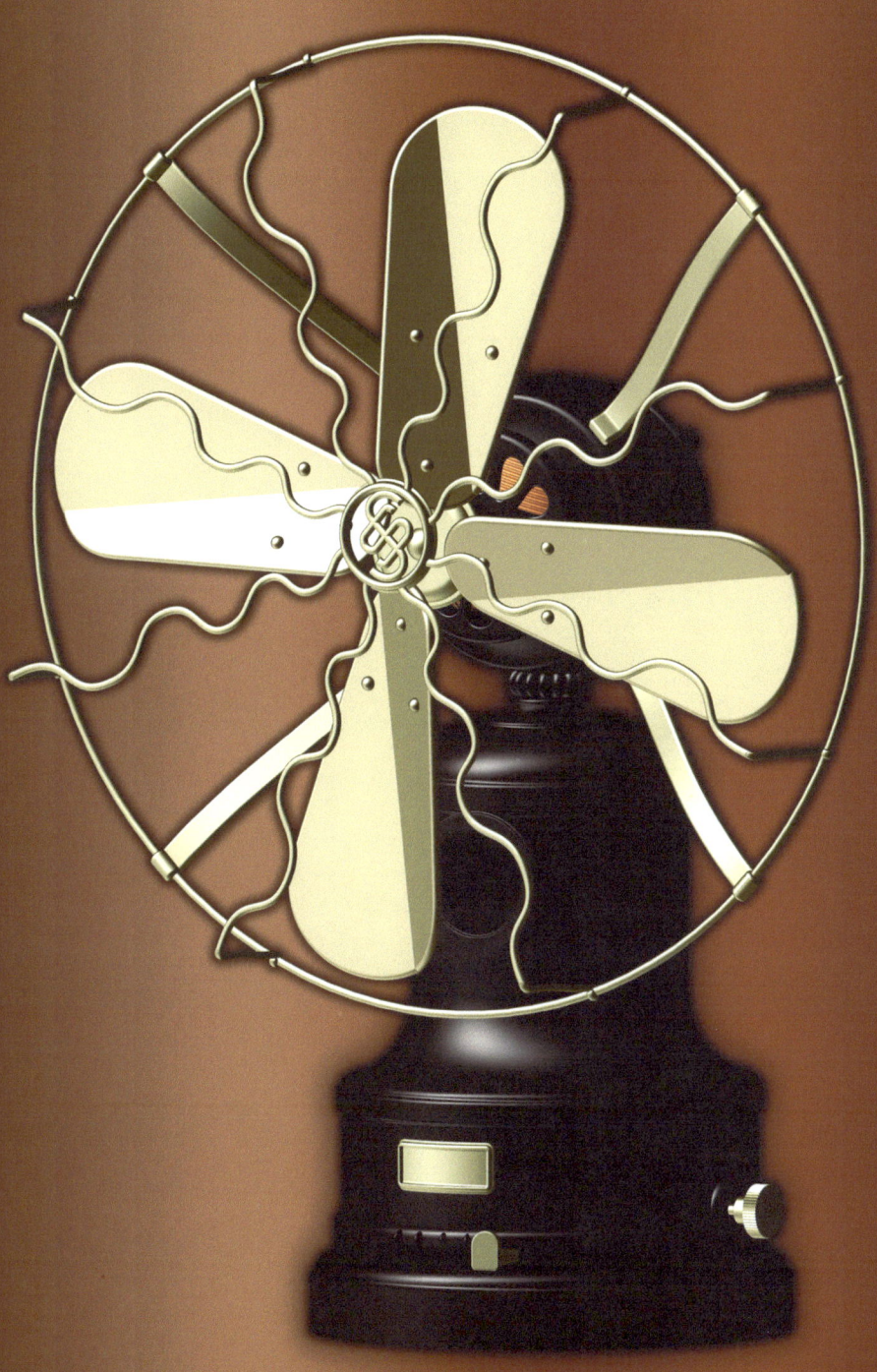

The button-down days of Madison Avenue in the turbulent 60s are recalled in the smooth sophistication of this sleek performer coated in rich satin grey crackle-finished steel. A one-piece, die-stamped aluminum blade reinforced with triple corrugations revolves around the reflector insignia with rocket streaming forth from a trio of vectors. A portent of the coming Space Age, perfect complement to a post-modern interior, and up-to-date household convenience facing a bright new future.

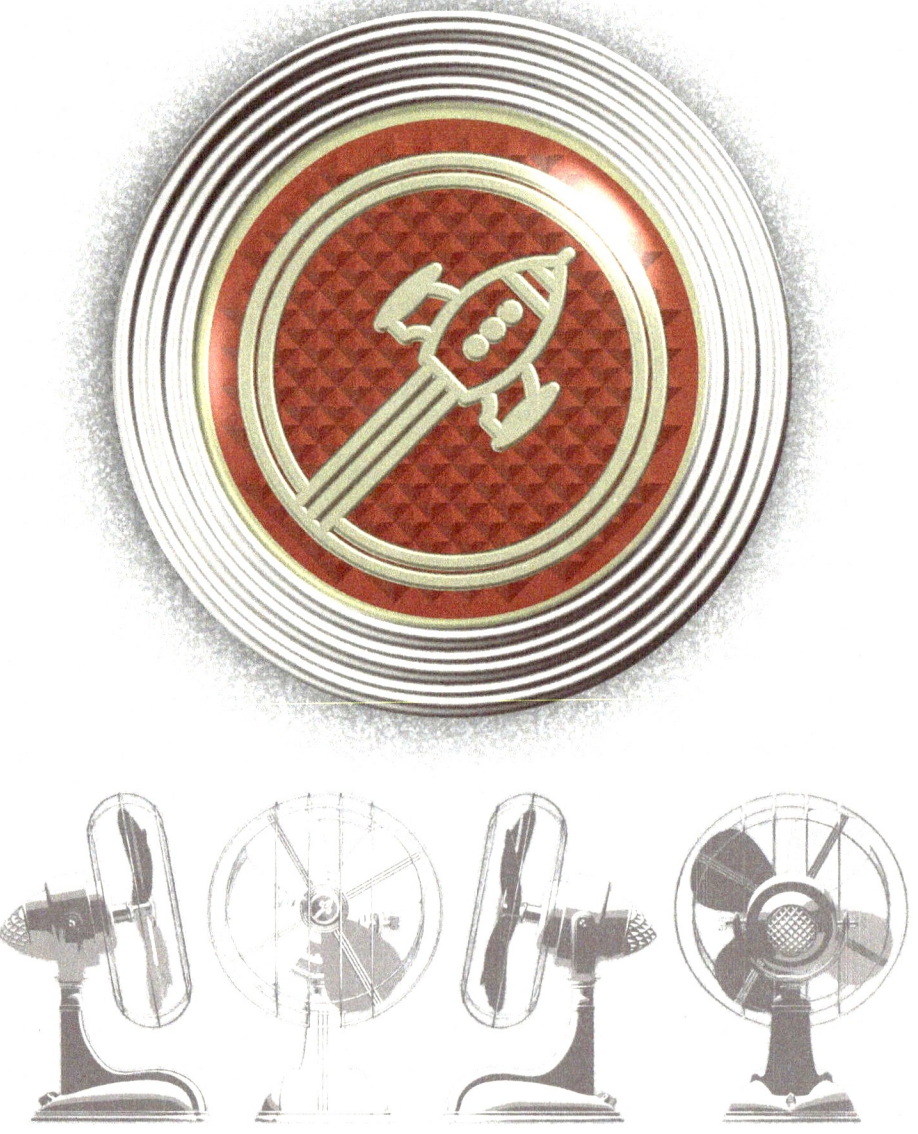

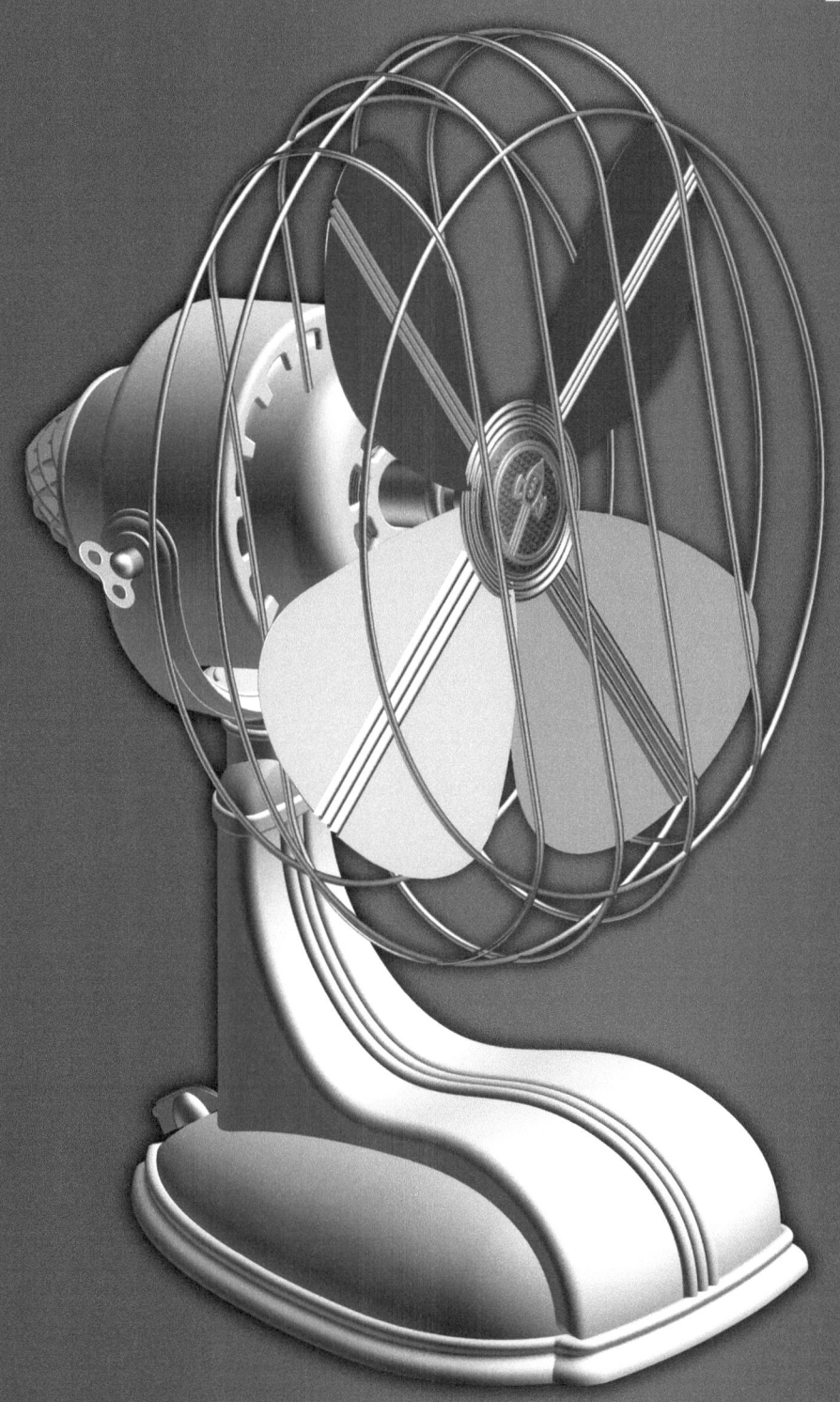

Flash Gordon, Commander Cody, Buck Rogers and so many of their ilk rode gleaming silver vessels through imaginary constellations for decades before the mysteries of deep space actually became ours to behold in earnest. The rocketship became a symbol of adventure, exploration and the final, yet undiscovered, frontier. A universal icon of power and triumph, reaching its zenith among the shining stars, it lent prestige to everything from automobiles to kitchen appliances as an assurance of our unfailing faith in progress. We, who came of age in these times of promise, believed in miracles and hope. We were then, and will be forever to come, the true rocket fans.

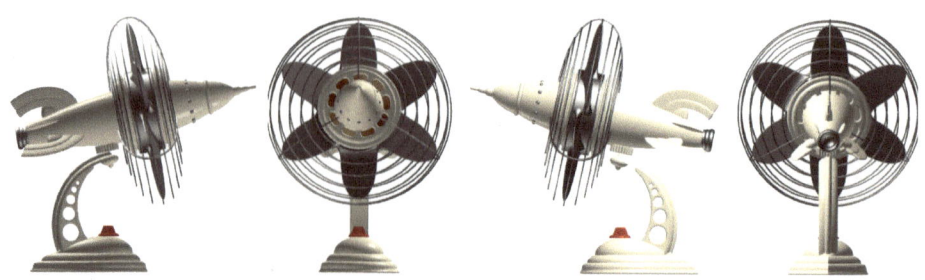

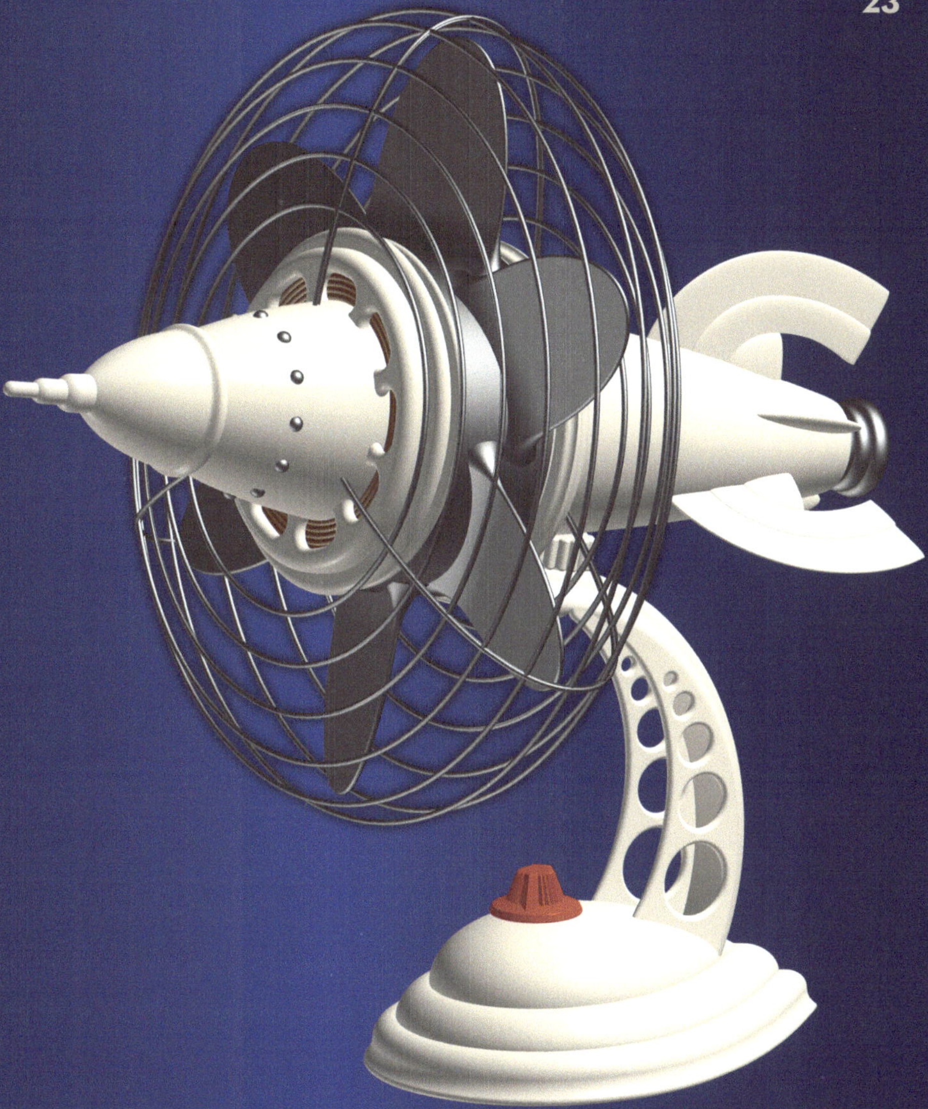

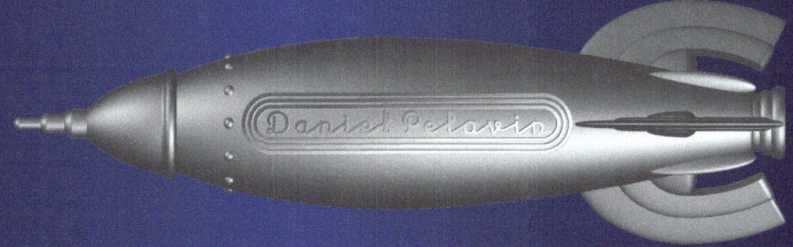

.

www.ingramcontent.com/pod-product-compliance
Lightning Source LLC
Chambersburg PA
CBHW040916180526
45159CB00010BA/3085